GRIZZLY BEARS

THERESA EMMINIZER

PowerKiDS
press

New York

Published in 2020 by The Rosen Publishing Group, Inc.
29 East 21st Street, New York, NY 10010

First Edition

Editor: Elizabeth Krajnik
Book Design: Reann Nye

Photo Credits: Cover, p. 10 Scott E Read/Shutterstock.com; pp. 5, 11, 18, 22 Dennis W Donohue/Shutterstock.com; p. 6 Daria Rybakova/Shutterstock.com; p. 7 by wildestanimal/Moment/Getty Images; p. 8 Kane513/Shutterstock.com; p. 9 Ian Stotesbury Photography/Moment/Getty Images; p. 12 Nick Dale / Design Pics/Getty Images; p. 13 Martin Rudlof Photography/Shutterstock.com. p. 14 Sergey Uryadnikov/Shutterstock.com; p. 15 Mike Korostelev www.mkorostelev.com/Moment/Getty Images; p. 17 Volodymyr Burdiak/Shutterstock.com; p. 19 Martin Mecnarowski/Shutterstock.com; p. 21 Kent Weakley/Shutterstock.com.

Library of Congress Cataloging-in-Publication Data

Names: Emminizer, Theresa, author.
Title: Grizzly bears / Theresa Emminizer.
Description: New York : PowerKids Press, [2020] | Series: Killers of the
    animal kingdom | Includes index.
Identifiers: LCCN 2019001188| ISBN 9781725306059 (paperback) | ISBN
    9781725306073 (library bound) | ISBN 9781725306066 (6 pack)
Subjects: LCSH: Grizzly bear–Juvenile literature.
Classification: LCC QL737.C27 E53 2020 | DDC 599.784–dc23
LC record available at https://lccn.loc.gov/2019001188

Manufactured in the United States of America

CPSIA Compliance Information: Batch #CSPK19. For Further Information contact Rosen Publishing, New York, New York at 1-800-237-9932.

CONTENTS

THE GREAT GRIZZLY

The grizzly bear is a kind of North American brown bear that lives in parts of Canada and the United States. Top predators armed with sharp claws, long teeth, and powerful **muscles**, these mighty animals have long been feared by humans. But are grizzly bears really as scary as they're made out to be? Is it possible that these animals are misunderstood?

To find out if these killers live up to their bad **reputation**, you'll need to take a closer look at how grizzly bears live in the wild. How do bears raise their young? What do they eat? How do they **behave**? Read on to find out!

KILLER FACTS

Grizzly bears got their name because of the **descriptions** written by late 18th and early 19th century explorers Edward Umfreville, Sir Alexander MacKenzie, Meriwether Lewis, and William Clark.

There are many **myths** about grizzly bears. It's important to sort out what's true and what's false.

5

A BEAR'S LIFE

Grizzly bears reach adulthood when they're about four years old. During late spring and early summer, adults come together to mate, or make babies. Baby grizzlies, which are called cubs, are born in January or February. At birth they weigh just one pound (0.45 kg).

KILLER FACTS

Male grizzly bears don't help females raise their cubs. While raising their young, mother bears are careful to stay away from males, who sometimes harm cubs.

Mother bears usually have two cubs at a time. However, they can have up to four cubs at a time.

Mother bears raise their cubs inside a den until April or May, when the cubs are strong enough to come out. Cubs will gain about 19 pounds (8.6 kg) before they're able to leave the den. Grizzly cubs stay with their mothers until they reach adulthood and, on average, can live to be 25 years old.

BEAR BEHAVIOR

Grizzly bears enter their den between October and December and stay inside until early spring. While inside their den, grizzly bears go into a deep sleep called torpor. During this time, the bear's heart rate and breathing slow and their body **temperature** drops a little. Torpor is different from hibernation because the bear can be awoken to fight off predators or give birth to its cubs.

During torpor, grizzly bears don't eat or go to the bathroom, and may lose up to 40 percent of their body weight. Males come out of their dens after about 131 days and females come out about 40 days later.

To get ready for torpor, grizzly bears eat up to 90 pounds (40.8 kg) of food a day.

9

BASIC BEAR FACTS

One reason grizzly bears got their name is because the long fur on their shoulders has silvery-gray tips. Grizzled means mixed with gray. Grizzly bears range in color from almost white to black, with many shades of brown in between. Some may be blond or even reddish-colored. A grizzly bear's color depends on what its parents look like.

When standing upright, grizzly bears can be up to 8 feet (2.4 m) tall!

Grizzly bears can weigh more than 700 pounds (317.5 kg). Male grizzlies are larger than females. Grizzly bears measure 3 to 3.5 feet (0.9 to 1.1 m) at shoulder height and are 6 to 7 feet (1.8 to 2.1 m) long.

WHAT DO THEY EAT?

Grizzly bears are apex predators. That means they're at the top of the food chain. They hunt large animals, such as elk, caribou, moose, mountain goats, and mountain sheep, as well as small animals, such as mice and salmon.

Although grizzlies spend much of their time alone, they come together in places where a lot of food can be found, such as rivers full of salmon.

Although they are powerful hunters, grizzly bears are omnivores, meaning they eat plants and animals. Grizzlies feed on nuts, berries, fruit, leaves, and roots. In some places where grizzly bears live, plants make up 80 to 90 percent of what they eat. Grizzly bears usually eat more during the summer and fall to build up fat so they can **survive** the cold winter inside their dens.

13

POWERFUL PREDATORS

Grizzly bears have a number of special skills that make them **fierce** hunters. Grizzly bears are fast runners and can reach speeds of up to 40 miles (64.4 km) per hour! They're also good swimmers and have sharp senses of hearing and smell. Grizzly bears can also climb trees, but they're not very good at it.

KILLER FACTS

As cubs, grizzly bears often climb trees. As they grow up, their long claws and heavy bodies make it harder for them to climb.

Grizzly bear claws are curved and can't be retracted, or pulled, into their paws.

Like other top predators, grizzly bears have long, sharp teeth they use to tear apart prey. Their claws, which are 2 to 4 inches (5.1 to 10.2 cm) long, help them dig small animals out of their underground homes and pull up roots.

15

WHERE DO THEY LIVE?

In the past, grizzly bears could be found from Alaska to Mexico and from California to Ohio. Today, they're found in fewer places. Grizzly bears can now be found in parts of western Canada, Alaska, Wyoming, Montana, Idaho, and Washington. They live in all sorts of **habitats**, including forests, woodlands, meadows, and **tundra**.

Grizzly bears keep to themselves and live in a home **range** that measures 10 to 380 square miles (25.9 to 984.2 sq km). They mark the **boundaries** of their range by rubbing against trees, leaving their scent behind. This may be a way to lessen fighting between adult male grizzlies.

KILLER FACTS

Between 1850 and 1970, the historic grizzly bear range shrank by 98 percent. Grizzly bear populations have dropped from as many as 50,000 to between 1,500 and 1,700.

There are about 150 grizzly bears with home ranges in Yellowstone National Park.

17

MAN vs. BEAR

For many years, grizzly bears have been thought of as monsters. In books, newspapers, and movies they are made out to be scary beasts that will kill you as soon as they see you. Seen as dangerous to people and **livestock**, grizzly bears were relentlessly hunted and killed during the 1800s. In addition to their vanishing habitats, hunting grizzlies shrank their population.

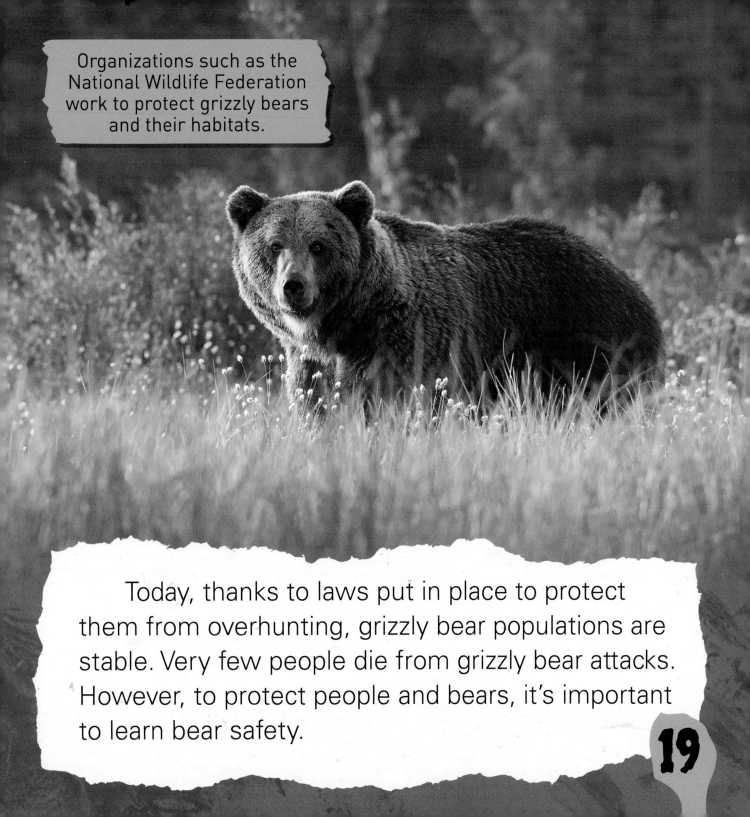

Today, thanks to laws put in place to protect them from overhunting, grizzly bear populations are stable. Very few people die from grizzly bear attacks. However, to protect people and bears, it's important to learn bear safety.

STAYING SAFE

Grizzly bears are shy and usually stay away from people. But if you do happen to cross paths with one, here are some tips to help you.

Never run away from a bear. Running will cause a bear to chase you, and you can't outrun a grizzly. Don't shoot a bear. Bears that are shot usually live long enough to harm their attackers. Bear spray, a spray designed to stop bears, is the best defense against grizzly attacks. Bear spray makes it hard for a bear to breathe, see, and smell for a short time, which gives you time to escape.

KILLER FACTS

Many people believe that a when a bear stands upright it's getting ready to attack. This isn't true! Bears usually stand upright to see things better. When they attack they do so on all fours.

BE BEAR AWARE

FOOD STORAGE REQUIRED

If you're camping in an area where grizzlies live, it's important to practice bear safety. Bears that want to eat your food may become dangerous.

ARE BEARS BEASTS?

Now that you know more about grizzly bears, do you think they're the monsters some people say they are, or are they simply misunderstood? Grizzly bears are important predators that are key to the health and balance of the **ecosystem**. Although grizzly attacks can be deadly, they don't happen often, and people can usually avoid them.

Most grizzly bear attacks happen when mother bears feel they need to protect their cubs. Understanding bear behavior and respecting their boundaries will prevent bear attacks. Keeping food and trash in sealed containers and practicing bear safety will make it possible for people and grizzlies to live together peacefully.

GLOSSARY

behave: To act in a particular way.

boundary: Something that marks the limit of an area or place.

description: Words that tell you how someone or something looks, sounds, etc.

ecosystem: A community of living things and the surroundings in which they live.

fierce: Likely to attack.

habitat: The surroundings where an animal or a plant naturally lives.

livestock: Farm animals.

muscle: A part of the body that produces motion.

myth: A story that people make up to explain events.

range: An area in which an animal lives.

reputation: The ideas people have about another person, an animal, or an object.

survive: To stay alive.

temperature: How hot or cold something is.

tundra: A cold, treeless plain with permanently frozen soil.

23

INDEX

WEBSITES

Due to the changing nature of Internet links, PowerKids Press has developed an online list of websites related to the subject of this book. This site is updated regularly. Please use this link to access the list: www.powerkidslinks.com/kotak/bears